MAKING
GOD KNOWN

Offering the

gift of life

YOUTH WITH A MISSION

ZondervanPublishingHouse
Grand Rapids, Michigan

A Division of HarperCollinsPublishers

GET CONNECTED!
Living Encounters Series

Making God Known
Copyright © 2000 by Youth With A Mission

Requests for information should be addressed to:

📖 ZondervanPublishingHouse
Grand Rapids, Michigan 49530

ISBN 0-310-22703-8

The Living Encounters Bible study series was produced through a dynamic team process of Youth With A Mission staff members, although each guide was created by one primary author. The team consisted of: Betty Barnett, Retha Badenhorst, Maureen Menard, Ruth Perrin, Ed Sherman, Donna Jo Taylor, and Christine Terrasson. The primary author of Making God Known *was Ed Sherman with contributions by Yan Nicholls.*

Interior design by Sherri Hoffman

Printed in the United States of America

99 00 01 02 03 04 05 /❖ EP/ 10 9 8 7 6 5 4 3 2 1

Contents

fOREWORD
Close Encounters with the Living God

Welcome to the Living Encounters Bible study series! We created this unique study to help sincere seekers find a deeper revelation of God. Our God loves to be pursued. He wants us to know and love him more, and there's no better way to learn of his character and his ways than through his written Word.

The Living Encounters series offers exciting new ways for you to engage Scripture and apply its truth to your life. Through this series, each participant is encouraged into living encounters with God, his Spirit, his Word, his people, and his world.

Some elements of the study are drawn from teaching methods that have been used for decades in our Discipleship Training Schools. As our students encounter God, their perspective on life changes radically. The very truth of the Scripture connects them to the global picture, to God's heart for the peoples of the world. Therefore, the more they come to know God, the more they want to make him known.

The Living Encounters series is a wonderful Bible study tool for people of various levels of spiritual maturity. Its flexible, user-friendly format appeals to people with different learning styles and cultural perspectives. And when coupled with the teaching aids found in the Christian Growth Study Bible (Zondervan), the series is a highly effective way to draw new understanding and guidance from the Scriptures.

May this series bring you a whole new appreciation of our awesome God—and set you on the pathway to many living encounters!

—Loren Cunningham,
Founder of Youth With A Mission

Introducing Living Encounters

Did you ever hear about a person you'd never met — what he said, what he looked like, what he did — and then you met him, and somehow the picture you had formed in your mind didn't fit at all? For better or worse, you were confronted with reality! An "encounter" does not mean a secondhand report about a person or a situation; it means a face-to-face meeting. In an encounter, you meet a person, and your knowledge about him or her combines with and adapts to the living reality.

This is what "Living Encounters" is all about. You have read God's Word, the Bible, but there is a gap between what it says and what you experience. You know God's Spirit is alive and well, but life would be a lot simpler if he sat down beside you and gave you advice. You like people, but sometimes loving them seems impossible. And then there's the whole world out there — so full of need and suffering that you don't know how to even begin to help.

Living Encounters are more than an analysis of Bible passages or a tool for group discussion. They are to help you *meet* and adjust your life to God's Word, God's Spirit, God's people, and God's world. They are designed to challenge you not only to grasp truth but to live it out, to connect it to your personal world and to the larger world around you. As you apply yourself to these studies, you can expect exciting changes both in your thinking and in your lifestyle.

The Living Encounters series is versatile. Each guide is divided into six sessions and can be used within a small-group discussion in a church or on a college campus. However, the series is designed so that it is just as effective for individual study.

The guides are personal. They constantly lead you to ask, "What does this mean to me and how do I apply it in my own life?" Questions reveal needs and desires of the heart and invite you to embrace the promises, assurances, exhortations, and challenges of God's Word. As you respond, the Spirit of God will be responding to you, renewing your mind and transforming you more into the likeness of Jesus Christ — the ultimate goal of all Bible study.

The Features

Each session includes the following basic features.

Opening Vignette

To draw you into the topic at hand, each session opens with a thought-provoking narrative.

Preparing Heart and Mind

These questions open your heart and focus your mind on what God wants to say to you in the passage. If you are using Living Encounters in a group setting, we strongly encourage you to include this section during the first fifteen minutes of your discussion. Please realize, however, that the entire study will probably take about an hour and fifteen minutes. If you don't have that much time, then ask your group members to reflect on these questions before you meet together, and begin your discussion with the section "Engaging the Text."

Setting the Stage

The background information found in this sidebar will help you better understand the context of the study.

Engaging the Text

This important section leads you through a Bible passage using inductive Bible study questions. The inductive method prompts you to observe, interpret, and apply the Bible passage with a variety of question styles:

- Observation questions will help you focus on what the Bible says.
- Interpretation questions will help you step into the world of the original readers to understand better what the passage meant to them.
- Application questions will help you to apply the truth to your heart and present circumstances.

Responding to God

In this section, you will receive suggestions that will help you focus your individual or group prayer time.

Punch Line

This brief sentence or verse will reinforce the theme of the session.

Taking It Further

This section is designed to be completed between studies to reinforce and further apply what you have learned. It offers a variety of suggestions for connecting what you have studied to your everyday life.

- **Connecting to Life**: a variety of activities to stimulate your personal growth and ministry to others.
- **Digging Deeper:** additional Scriptures to give a deeper and broader understanding of what the Bible says about the topic of the study.
- **Meditation:** a time to reflect more deeply on a specific verse or passage.
- **Personal Expression:** creative suggestions to help you process and apply what you've learned in the session.
- **World Focus:** an encouragement to look beyond your personal realm to the needs of our world.

Additional Features

In addition to the above, the guides contain a variety of optional features. All are designed to appeal to different learning styles and gifts and to encourage deeper integration of material into all of life. It is expected that you will choose whatever features you find most useful for each session. These optional features, found in articles throughout the sessions, include:

- Gray boxed material: often these will be devotional articles relevant to the study.
- People of Impact: a snapshot of the life of a person who models the principles studied.
- People Profile: a brief description of a people group that needs to be reached with the gospel.
- Hot Topic: a discussion starter to use with other group members to stimulate deeper thinking on a difficult subject.

Leader's Notes

Leader's notes for each session are provided at the back of each study guide.

Suggestions for Individual or Group Study

Preparing Heart and Mind

1. Ask the Lord for insight, wisdom, and grace to understand the Bible passage and apply it to your own life.
2. Choose one or more of the preparation questions and take time to think about it.

Engaging the Text

1. Read and reread the assigned Bible passage. You may find it helpful to have several different translations. A good literal translation rather than a paraphrase is recommended, such as the *New International Version*, the *New American Standard Bible*, the *New Revised Standard Version*, and the *New King James Bible*. The questions in each study are based on the *New International Version*. A Bible dictionary can also serve you well for look-

ing up any unfamiliar words, people, places, or theological concepts. Commentaries, while having great value, are not part of this kind of study, which uses the inductive method.

2. The questions are designed to help you make observations, draw conclusions, and apply God's truth to your life. Write your answers in the space provided. Recording your observations and conclusions is an important step in any study process. It encourages you to think through your answers thoroughly, thus furthering the learning process.

3. Note the optional elements offered in the sidebars. These are designed to encourage greater understanding of the passage being studied.

4. Be aware of the continuous presence of the Lord throughout the process. You may want to stop and pray in the midst of your study. Be sure to end your study with a time of waiting, listening, and responding to the Lord in prayer.

5. Be willing to participate in the discussion. The leader of the group will not be lecturing; rather, he or she will be encouraging the members of the group to discuss what they have learned from the passage. The leader will be asking the questions that are found in this guide. Plan to share what God has taught you in your individual study time.

6. Stick to the passage being studied. Your answers should be based on the verses which are the focus of the discussion and not on outside authorities such as commentators or speakers (or the commentary notes in your study Bible!).

7. Be sensitive to other members of the group. Listen attentively when they share. You can learn a lot from their insights! Stick with the topic — when you have insights on a different subject, keep it for another time so the group is not distracted from the focus of the study.

8. Be careful not to dominate the discussion. We are sometimes so eager to share that we leave too little opportunity for others to contribute. By all means participate, but allow others to do so as well.

9. Expect the Holy Spirit to teach you both through the passage and through other members of the group. Everyone has a unique perspective that can broaden your own understanding. Pray that you will have an enjoyable and profitable time together.
10. The "Responding to God" section is the place where you pray about the topics you have studied. At this time you will invite the Holy Spirit to work these truths further into each of your lives. Be careful not to overlook this essential aspect of your time together.

Taking It Further

1. Identify other questions that arise through the study so that you can pursue them later.
2. Choose one or more of the activities to help you apply the principles in your life. These are optional activities to be done on your own after the Bible study session.

Leader's Notes

If you are the discussion leader or simply want further information, you will find additional suggestions and ideas for each session in the Leader's Notes in the back of the book.

Making God Known:
Offering the Gift of Life

Dave loves to talk to other people about his God. He gladly shares during lunch breaks at work, with someone sitting beside him on a plane, or with a new friend he has made—anywhere that his life touches those who don't yet know Jesus.

But it wasn't always this way. Dave used to think that an evangelist was either a Billy Graham preaching before thousands, or someone shouting unnoticed on a street corner. He knew he would never become the one, and he couldn't stand the idea of being the other. If those were the options, then being an evangelist was out for him. Even worse, some well-meaning Christians said that if he didn't share the gospel, people would go to hell. Guilt would rise in his heart, but guilt wasn't a good motivator.

Then one day a totally new perspective on evangelism opened up to him. Reading Paul's letter to the Corinthians, a little phrase caught his attention: "For Christ's love compels us" (2 Corinthians 5:14). *Of course!* he thought. It wasn't guilt which had motivated Paul, but Christ's love for the lost! Realizing how little of such love he had, Dave prayed that God would change his heart.

Something else encouraged Dave. A speaker at church asked who had met Christ at an evangelistic campaign. Expecting a forest of hands to rise with his own, Dave was puzzled when only a few did. The response was the same when the speaker inquired who had done so through reading a gospel tract. By this time Dave was really curious. Then the man asked the congregation who had come to Christ through a friend or family member sharing with them. A sea of hands waved across the auditorium. The speaker wasn't at all surprised. "You will find the same thing in almost any gathering of Christians," he told them.

With a sense of freedom and relief, Dave's view of evangelism changed radically. He could simply talk about the God he loved with those he knew and met in the course of daily life! And God answered his prayer. His love grew for those who did not yet know Christ. Talking with them in his normal manner, Dave found that opportunities rose naturally to share. Dave is not an "evangelist," but is now effective in sharing his faith and leading many into a relationship with the living God.

Like Dave, many of us have had a negative view of evangelism. We feel it is too high a calling, or poor examples have put us off. Guilt *de*motivates us. But God intends evangelism to be a natural sharing of the gift of life that we have received from him. And our most effective witness for Christ will be to those we know, who not only hear our words but see our lives as well.

This study offers practical tips in sharing your faith, as well as an understanding of what the Bible says about evangelism. It clarifies what the gospel is in this day of confusing messages. If you desire a greater compassion for the lost, more confidence in sharing your faith effectively right where you are, and a bigger picture of what God is doing in the world . . .

. . . then this study is for you!

God's Heart for the Lost
Luke 19:1–10

It was late when Ed set off down the chilly street to his car. He hardly noticed the drunk lying in the sidewalk until in his heart he heard God say, "Go back and tell him that I love him." Ed pushed on. "That can't be the Lord; it's just me," he told himself. But the voice was insistent. Ed struggled, then gave in. He turned back to the man and told him of God's love. Realizing that it really was a cold night, he knew he couldn't leave the man lying there. It was obvious he didn't have money, so Ed helped him to find a room and paid for the night for him.

It's so easy not to notice the lost people we encounter. But God sees them. And he wants us to share his heart of compassion for them. We aren't to reach out to the lost because we feel sorry for them, or because we feel guilty if we don't. God loves them, and it must be his love that motivates us to action. We can ask him to give us his heart for those who do not know him. Without him, they are lost. Without him, they can never change. He is the one who seeks people out and changes their hearts. And he uses you and me to do that.

> **"For the Son of Man came to seek and to save what was lost."**
>
> —Luke 19:10

Not all of us are evangelists. Ed certainly isn't. But we can all learn to sense God's heart and to reach out with *his* love to the world around us. As you begin this study, ask the Holy Spirit to give you more of his heart for the lost.

- How do you think God feels about the drunk on *your* street (or the lost, greedy businessman next door)?

- Can you think of someone you would be willing to die for? Why?

enGaGinG the text

setting the stage

- Jesus is on his way to Jerusalem, where he will be crucified by the Roman authorities at the instigation of the Jewish leadership.

- The Jews view tax collectors as collaborators with the occupying Romans. Tax collectors are therefore hated by their fellow countrymen.

- The Romans assign a sum that a tax collector must collect in any district. Anything accumulated above that amount is for their own salary. Many abuse this arrangement to enrich themselves at the expense of their fellow citizens.

- Jesus is known as a friend of tax collectors, acknowledged sinners, and other socially unacceptable people.

- Hospitality is very important in first-century Palestine. Whether giving or receiving, it implies a kind of identification with the other.

Read Luke 19:1–10

1. Jesus is on his way to Jerusalem to die for the sins of the world, yet he takes the time to reach out to one lost tax collector. What does this tell you about Jesus' priorities?

2. Identify an opportunity that you have had to share the gospel with someone, but because of your own busyness, troubles, or even insecurity, you passed it up. Describe it.

3. Consider the various things Zacchaeus does to see Jesus. What does this tell you about his desire to see Jesus? Why do you think Zacchaeus wants to see Jesus? (See also Setting the Stage.)

For Even One

Read Acts 8:5–8; 26–27.

God isn't just concerned with saving the masses; he will do everything possible to rescue even one lost individual. As we carry out our evangelism practices, we need this commitment too. We see it in Philip (Acts 8), who preached to the crowds, yet ran to catch a chariot for the sake of one person.

These qualities are also evident in the life of evangelist Billy Graham. He once returned to his hotel after leading hundreds to a relationship with Jesus Christ. In the hallway a drunk man exclaimed, "Well, if it isn't Billy Graham, the world's number one rip-off artist!" Billy invited the man to his room for a cup of tea, and by 3 A.M. the man had sobered up and given his heart to Jesus.

A heart of love for both God and others is the most important thing we need to draw others to Jesus. Philip, the only person in the Bible referred to as an evangelist, beautifully modeled this lifestyle of love.

Will you risk stepping out to follow God's promptings for the sake of one person?

4. Think about the sort of man Zacchaeus is (v. 8; Setting the Stage). What is the significance of Jesus going to his home for a meal?

5. What would motivate Jesus to risk his reputation in this way?

6. Think of a time when you risked your reputation to reach out to someone lost who was disliked by people around you. What motivated you?

Do you think that the people's evaluation of Zacchaeus was fair? (See Setting the Stage.)

Mission of Redemption

"The Spirit of the Lord is on me, because he has anointed me to preach good news to the poor. He has sent me to proclaim freedom for the prisoners and recovery of sight for the blind, to release the oppressed, to proclaim the year of the Lord's favor" (Luke 4:18–19).

In declaring that he was the fulfillment of this prophecy from Isaiah 61:1–2, Jesus asserted to all people, for all time, that he is the answer to every human need. He spent the next three years demonstrating this truth: bringing hope, freedom, and healing to the spiritually poor and broken. Now he is asking us to bring his message of hope to hurting people.

Kirsten was one of those hurting people. At age twenty-two, she had a live-in lover and a good-paying job at an abortion clinic, but inwardly she felt miserable. An added frustration was having to pass through—and sometimes evict—the protesters who regularly gathered outside the clinic. Mostly, Kirsten avoided eye contact, but one day she noticed that a couple of them were smiling and talking to her directly. Soon their genuine warmth and kindness broke through her suspicions—and friendships began to develop. Their acceptance of her, in spite of the work she did, led Kirsten to think again about the clinic's objectives. In her mind's eye she began to see babies appear on the sonogram screens instead of blobs, and she found herself encouraging patients *not* to have abortions. Eventually, she found a whole new life of joy and freedom in Jesus Christ.

The wonderful truth of the gospel is that it is Good News! The more guilty and broken a person is, the more gentle Jesus is with them. Guilt-producing remarks didn't win Kirsten to Christ; love and kindness did.

Do you know someone who needs God's unconditional love? What will you do to share it?

7. Why might their opinion of him change through what happens?

8. What is the main difference between the way Jesus treats Zacchaeus and the way the crowd initially treats him?

9. Why do you think Jesus doesn't wait for Zacchaeus to change before he befriends him?

10. Should we expect lost people to change *before* we show them God's love? Explain your answer.

People sometimes say that God's love is unconditional. Yet Zacchaeus does not respond to Jesus by simply receiving his acceptance and remaining as he is, but by generous giving and restitution. What is the relationship between good works and our salvation?

11. What keeps us from befriending more people like Zacchaeus?

In what ways do you expect other people to change before you are willing to associate with them?

12. In what ways would you like your life to more truly reflect the heart of God for the world?

RESPONDING to GOD

Spend time in prayer thanking God that he reached out to you in his love. Ask him to give you a greater measure of love for those who do not yet know him.

while we were still sinners, christ died for us.

Romans 5:8

taking it furtheR

Suggestions for application

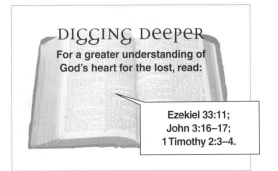

DIGGING DEEPER

For a greater understanding of God's heart for the lost, read:

Ezekiel 33:11;
John 3:16–17;
1 Timothy 2:3–4.

Personal Expression

Cut a large heart out of red paper, representing God's heart. Decorate it as much as you would like to make it attractive (as God's heart is). Ask God to remind you of people in your network of relationships who don't yet know him. Put the heart in a place where you will see it each day, and pray regularly that God will give you more of his heart for these people. Be prepared for him to show you practical ways to express that love.

Meditation

Read through Romans 5:6–11. Identify different aspects of God's character found in these verses. Think about what these characteristics of God have meant to you. Ask the Holy Spirit to show you ways in which you can view the lost from God's perspective, as reflected in these verses.

WORLD FOCUS

Think of a world leader in the news who does not "deserve" God's mercy. Pray for this leader, that God would meet and change him or her. You may need to ask God to change your heart toward this person first! Using the "Principles for Effective Intercession" on pages 101–2 may be helpful.

tHE Best News Ever
1 Corinthians 15:1–28

Jayne was only nineteen, but she was already feeling old. There didn't seem to be much she hadn't tried, and it had all been fun at first. Slowly, however, everything had become less and less satisfying, leaving her feeling empty and unfulfilled. If only she could start all over again!

A Christian at work named Mary had befriended her. Jayne didn't think they had much in common, but she found she enjoyed chatting with Mary. She didn't condemn the sin in Jayne's life, but took time to listen to her and occasionally mentioned what Jesus had done for her. Most of Mary's religious talk didn't mean much to her, but one day Mary talked about Jesus saying that a person must be born again (John 3:3). Jayne interrupted. "Is that really possible—to have a new start?" she asked, interested. Mary explained further, and Jayne eventually asked Jesus to give her a new beginning. The gospel had at last become good news for her!

I am not ashamed of the gospel.

—ROMANS 1:16

Many people do not see the gospel as "good news" (which is what the word "gospel" means). Some get the impression that to be a Christian means having to follow a long set of rules. For some, accepting the gospel would mean rejection by their families. But the gospel of Jesus Christ is the best news ever! Part of our responsibility in sharing it with others is to help them see how it is good news for them. For Jayne, it meant that she could start life over again. For some it means an end to the fear of death that haunts them. The gospel message must be able to enter each individual's real, everyday world and demonstrate that it is "good news." For that reason Scripture speaks of it in different ways: being born again; the forgiveness of sins; the defeat of Satan.

The passage in Corinthians which we are about to look at is one of the most comprehensive in explaining what the gospel, in all its richness, is about. As you begin this study, ask the Holy Spirit to enlarge your understanding and experience of what *good news* it is.

PREPARING HEART AND MIND

- When someone tells you that there's good news for you, what thoughts or emotions come to mind?

- In your own words, explain what the gospel means to you.

- When people look at you, do they see "good news" or "bad news"?

engaging the text

setting the stage

- Corinth is an important commercial city in Greece in the time of Paul.

- Immorality is common among Gentile pagans, involving idolatry and temple prostitution. The early church in Corinth is composed mostly of Gentile believers, who are still influenced by their immoral background.

- Some teachers are denying that the dead will be raised. This is probably an influence of the dualism in Greek thought, which claims that physical matter is inherently evil while spirit is inherently good.

- "Dominion, authority and power" (1 Corinthians 15:24) are terms the New Testament uses to describe demonic beings (see also Ephesians 6:12).

- The message preached by Jesus, and later by the apostles and the early church, is frequently called the "gospel of the kingdom." "Kingdom" means the rule or reign of God.

Read 1 Corinthians 15:1–28

1. What are the essential elements of the gospel that Paul lays out in this passage? (See especially verses 3–8, 9–11, 20, 23–28.)

2. Why does Paul say that these things are "of first importance" (v. 3)?

3. Consider when you first became a Christian. What was it about the gospel message that made it "good news" to you?

How has your appreciation for the goodness of its message grown since then?

Message in the Stars

How do we demonstrate God's existence to an unbeliever? The best evidence is all around us. The vastness and orderliness of the universe make it impossible to believe that it happened because of some random cosmic explosions.

Consider the density of the stars. Scientists think our galaxy, the Milky Way, contains about 100 billion stars. But our galaxy is only one among millions, if not billions. Psalm 19 observes that night after night these stars pour forth speech to "declare the glory of God."

An Eastern mystic named Rabi Maharaj actually came to faith in Jesus Christ through thinking about creation. In his book *Death of a Guru*, he says he once believed that creation was God and God was creation. One day he was struck by this thought: How could the creation create itself? He then prayed: "God the Creator, please show me the truth," which led to the guru's conversion.

In evangelism, we need to make sure that people believe in an uncreated Creator before we proceed to other truths (see article on "World Religions and Cults," page 00). Because God has so wonderfully shown his nature and love in creation, let us point others to this powerful evidence!

What aspects of creation most clearly show you the glory of God?

4. From this passage in 1 Corinthians 15, describe what Christ has done and what God expects of you in response.

What Christ has done (vv. 3–8; 9–10a; 24–28):

Your response (vv. 1–2; 10b–11; 24–26):

5. Paul speaks of grace in a very dynamic way. Identify at least two aspects of grace he mentions in verses 9–11. How does your own understanding and experience of grace compare with what Paul says here?

6. As you consider this, identify ways in which you would like to grow in your own experience of grace.

7. What is it about the resurrection of Jesus that makes it so central to our faith (vv. 20–22)?

8. Some Christians have said that even if it was only for this life, it is worth knowing Jesus and being a Christian. Compare Paul's view of this (vv. 18–19) with your own.

9. In verse 24, Paul speaks of Christ destroying "dominion, authority and power" — that is, Satan and his rule in this world (see Setting the Stage). What makes this part of our message good news? Do you know of any examples where the power of Christ has defeated demonic power in people's lives, either in your own or in others? Describe one.

10. Paul concludes this portion of his discussion on the Resurrection with an overview of human history, from Adam's fall and its consequences to the glorious end in the future. In light of what he says, what are the implications of the Resurrection:

   • for you personally, both now and into eternity?

   • for the whole world, both now and into eternity?

11. What changes might you need to make in your life and attitudes in order to participate more fully in the picture Paul is describing?

Go Teach It to the Nations!

In Jesus' final instructions he urged his followers to preach the gospel to every person (Mark 16:15–19) and to make disciples of every nation (Matthew 28:18–20). He wanted those who were being baptized to be instructed in *all* the ways of God, so that the life-giving transformation of the gospel would be experienced both in the heart of the individual and in the corporate expression of every people group.

The work of the cross affects all areas of life touched by sin. All things will be reconciled to God through Jesus (2 Corinthians 5:18; Colossians 1:20). The teachings of Jesus apply therefore to every aspect of life—to our education, our finances, our sexuality, our families, our communication, our government, and every other influential area. The gospel is like the yeast that Jesus described in Matthew 13:33. When it gets into society, it should influence everything!

Down through the centuries, Christians have made huge contributions to the fields of science, education, the arts, medicine, government, and many others. And as we continue to call men and women of every nation to faith in Jesus Christ, we should expect the influence of his righteousness and creativity to grow. As believers, we must not abandon certain professions and places of influence because of the darkness there. Those are the very places where God wants to shine the light of Jesus!

What areas of society have you felt were beyond the influence of the gospel? Ask God for eyes of faith as you pray for these areas.

Thank God for "such a great salvation" (Hebrews 2:3). Ask him to help you live out and share your salvation in such a way that others will see that it is also truly "good news" for them.

it is the power of god for the salvation of everyone who believes.

Romans 1:16

taking it further
Suggestions for application

DIGGING DEEPER

For more insight on what the Bible has to say about the gospel, read:

Psalm 51; Matthew 4:23; John 4:13–14; Acts 20:24; Ephesians 2:1–10.

Personal Expression

Write a story as if it were for a newspaper, with an appropriate headline, telling the gospel that Paul describes in these verses from Corinthians. Use "quotations" from the eyewitnesses he mentions.

Connecting to Life

Identify ways in which your manner of sharing the gospel might change or broaden as a result of this study. Ask God to give you an opportunity to put it into practice with at least one person this week.

WORLD FOCUS

Read about the people group, the Bhils, on the next two pages, and take time to pray for them. Refer to "Prayer Strategies for Changing Nations," pages 103–5, for helpful guidelines.

PEOPLE PROFILE

the BHILS—IN search of safe passage to eternity

Location: India, Pakistan. Population: 8 million. Religion: 95% Animist.

Jukria lay awake all night worrying about his father. All the funeral rites had been observed: Consecrated fire was taken to the burial site; holy water was sprinkled; and food offerings of bread and rice were lovingly placed where Taraji could reach them. Jukria was careful to tear the custom-dictated small hole in the burial shroud. Each day's rituals were meticulously observed by the whole family. Yet Jukria still worried.

He lay nervously awaiting the dawn. This would be the twelfth day since Taraji had died, a day critical to his safe passage to heaven. Jukria had engaged a wise old *Brahman* (Hindu priest) to chant the day's prayers. But late in the night the message had come that the *Brahman* was ill, and his novice would take his place. Jukria knew that if Taraji were still alive, he would be furious that a novice should officiate on such a critical day. But what to do? The ceremonies had to go ahead.

In his mind Jukria rehearsed the day's rituals. They all had to be right—for his father's destiny was at stake. As eldest son Jukria was responsible to ensure that his father's soul passed safely into heaven. This was the day the *chodhvan* (a seven-step ladder) would be erected, and as the novice sat beneath it, chanting verses from the *Puranas* (scriptures), Taraji's soul would climb into heaven.

Knots twisted in Jukria's stomach as he fought unwanted thoughts. Would Taraji's soul refuse to climb the ladder when he saw the novice? Would Taraji remain on earth forever as a ghost? Jukria lay alone in the dark, wishing there was assurance of the afterlife.

Pray that:
- The Bhils would come to the knowledge of the truth that God desires all people to be saved (1 Timothy 2:4).
- The Holy Spirit would stir dissatisfaction in the Bhils concerning the emptiness of the endless rituals they feel duty-bound to perform.
- The Bhils would understand that "relationship," not "ritual," is the key to eternal life with God.

Prayer—Preparing the Way
Acts 4:23–37; 5:12–16

"*Khmer Rouge torturer now Christian evangelist.*" The headline caught Sue's eye. Her excitement grew as she read how the infamous Kang Kek Ieu, known in Cambodia by his nickname "Duch," had become a Christian. As the head of the Cambodian secret police, he had assisted in bringing about the murder of hundreds of thousands of his own people. Now he had accepted Jesus Christ as his Savior. But he was not seeking to use his faith as a means of escaping punishment. Instead, he freely admitted that he had done "terrible things" and courageously declared himself willing to face trial for his actions.

The reason for Sue's excitement was not only that such an infamous man had turned to Christ. She was remembering that almost twenty years before, at the height of the murders in Cambodia, she and a group of other Christians had prayed daily for "Duch." They had not known him by name, but she and her friends had prayed for God to reach out in mercy to those committing such horrendous crimes and draw them to himself, that they would know that Jesus' death had made forgiveness possible, even for them. And now, years later, Duch had responded to the love of God.

I urge . . . that prayers . . . be made for everyone.

—1 timothy 2:1

Perhaps no one you are praying for has sunk so deeply into sin and evil as Duch had, but God always uses our prayer to prepare the way for his gospel to reach hearts. Through prayer we become partners with God in what he is doing to win the lost to himself. Sue knew that although she had not been the one to share the gospel directly with Duch, she had had a part in preparing the way to his heart.

As we look at the early church in prayer and action, ask the Holy Spirit to use this study to motivate you and increase your faith in praying diligently for those who don't yet know Christ.

PREPARING heart and mind

- Who do you pray for that needs to be changed by the gospel?

- In what ways would you like to see your prayers for the lost deepen?

engaging the text

setting the stage

- This passage in Acts is set in the very early days of the church, probably only weeks after the first Pentecost.

- Peter and John have just healed a lame man and been arrested for preaching in the name of Jesus (Acts 3:1–4:22). They are released after being instructed not to preach in Jesus' name again.

- Their response to this is: "Judge for yourselves whether it is right in God's sight to obey you rather than God. For we cannot help speaking about what we have seen and heard" (Acts 4:19).

Read Acts 4:23–37

1. What has just happened before this time of prayer (see Setting the Stage)?

2. What are some important elements in the prayer (vv. 24–30)?

3. The people describe God in a number of different ways as they pray. What are these?

4. Why are these elements (referred to in Questions 2 and 3) important to remember when you pray for the lost?

5. How do *you* pray for family and friends who don't yet know Christ? Compare this with the elements of the prayer in this passage.

   - What are the similarities?

   - What are the differences?

Quoting Scripture

Note how the people quote Scripture as part of their prayers. They thus "proclaim" truth before God, while at the same time reminding themselves of his Word. We too can use appropriate Scripture passages as we pray to help us speak out truth and build up our faith.

6. In their prayer the people identify what *God* has done. What do they ask that *they* can do?

7. Why do we need to pray for the lost to understand the gospel when we do evangelism? (See also 2 Corinthians 4:3; 10:5.)

8. Can you think of a time when you prayed before you shared the gospel and it made a difference? Describe it.

9. Verse 31 describes a dramatic event following the time of prayer. Why does God fill them with the Holy Spirit?

Why would you want God to fill *you* with the Holy Spirit?

Prepare with Prayer

Evangelism cannot be simply an exercise in communication. To be at all effective, it must be a work of the Spirit released through prayer.

Frustrated leaders of a fledging church in the Philippines turned to prayer to find out why no one was responding to their message. The Lord led them to follow the guidance of Isaiah 62:7 and "give him no rest" until he established his work there. They formed a round-the-clock prayer vigil that lasted over a month. Near the end of it, a number of young people accepted Jesus as Savior, and from those converts came some of the ministry's future leaders.

Any efforts of strategic evangelism are largely a waste of time without prayer. In prayer, we receive vital insights into how most effectively to communicate the gospel to our targeted group. Prayer helps us to feel God's love for them and prepares our hearts to speak his message. Prayer thwarts the enemy's plans to interrupt, confuse, and discourage our efforts. And finally, prayer releases God's Spirit to go before us and prepare the people we will meet to receive the good news of life in Jesus.

Are you praying for God to open evangelism opportunities for you? Ask him how you can pray for your nation.

10. Verses 32–37 describe the life of the early church together. In what ways might such a lifestyle help fulfill their desire to see the lost saved?

11. The early church prays, and the quality of their life together changes as a consequence. Can you think of a time that this has happened to you or within your church? Describe it.

Alike on the Inside

On a passing bus in the city of Amsterdam, Landa noticed a little old lady, gray hair in a neatly groomed bun, seated next to a young man with spiked hair that was dyed fiery red. The Holy Spirit whispered, "You see those people as different, don't you?" Landa almost laughed aloud. But her amusement turned to shock when she heard the Lord say, "I don't see any difference in them at all."

Focusing on external differences will always cause us to feel alienated from those whose looks and backgrounds differ from our own. We all are sinners equally in need of grace. In our work of evangelism, the Holy Spirit will challenge us to grab hold of the similarities we share with our fellow human beings, created in God's image, and to meet them on that common ground.

Once we begin living this reality—by being friendly and kind to people who are different—the Lord will open plenty of opportunities for us to communicate his love.

What kinds of people do you shy away from? Do you see them as unreachable? If so, ask God how to communicate his Good News with them.

Read Acts 5:12–16

12. In what ways do you see a fulfillment of the church's earlier prayer in these verses?

13. Do you know of someone who was healed or had some other supernatural experience with God (such as a vision or dream) that brought the person to the Lord? Describe it.

14. What have you learned from studying these passages that you would like to incorporate into your own prayer life?

RESPONDING TO GOD

Think of someone you know who is in need of the gospel. Keeping in mind your response to Question 14, take time to pray for the person. As you pray, consciously apply what you have learned.

they should always pray and not give up.

Luke 18:1

taking it further
Suggestions for application

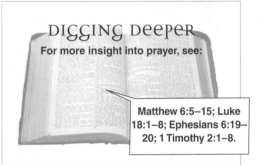

DIGGING DEEPER
For more insight into prayer, see:

Matthew 6:5–15; Luke 18:1–8; Ephesians 6:19–20; 1 Timothy 2:1–8.

Connecting to Life

Pray daily this week that God will give you an opportunity to share your faith with someone who is not yet a believer, and then look for the opportunity you prayed for. In addition to what you've learned in this study, you may find "Principles for Effective Intercession" (pages 101–2) helpful.

Meditation

Consider the life of Nicolas von Zinzendorf (page 45), whose passion and prayer for the lost helped pioneer the modern missionary movement. Write down ways that his example and that of the early Moravians he led speak to you.

WORLD FOCUS

Pray for a world leader in the news this week who is in need of God. You may find it helpful to refer to the "Principles for Effective Intercession" on pages 101–2.

PEOPLE OF IMPACT

NICOLAS VON ZINZENDORF (1700–1760)

Passionate Prayer, Ready Sacrifice

All eyes in the room turned to Count Nicolas von Zinzendorf, scanning his features for a reaction to the two men's shocking proposal. They had just volunteered to sell themselves as slaves in order to take the gospel to the plantations of the West Indies!

The German nobleman could never have imagined when he offered refuge to Moravian Christians fleeing religious persecution that his decision would help spark such radical faith. In 1727, spiritual renewal swept through the growing refugee community at his Herrnhut estate. So great was the Moravians' passion for prayer that they started a round-the-clock prayer vigil that continued unabated for over one hundred years.

The second great moment of Count Zinzendorf's destiny came when he met a slave from the West Indies. The slave pleaded for missionaries to reach out to his people, and when the Count returned to Herrnhut, he challenged the Moravians to reach them for Jesus Christ. The Moravians' wholehearted response pioneered the modern missionary movement.

Count Zinzendorf championed and financed missions for thirty-three years, launching Moravians into service in the Americas, Africa, Europe, and Greenland. Although born and bred for a life of royalty and ease, he chose to sacrificially serve Jesus Christ, working tirelessly as a missionary statesman. His one great regret, which he realized at his wife's death, was the destruction he had brought to his own family through his inattentiveness to them as he gave himself so completely to his work. Yet he did leave this legacy: sending out self-supporting laypeople as evangelists. Considered radical at the time, this principle is widely applied today.

Sharing Your testimony
Acts 26:1–29

George was tired of sharing his testimony. He had been involved in a lot of darkness—drugs, theft, the occult—and Jesus had broken into his life in an amazing way. Other Christians loved to hear his story. But there was much more to his life than his "testimony." A Christian for two years, he wanted people to know who he was *now* in Christ, not just who he had been. Yet one day when he was asked to share his testimony in a group of new friends, a non-Christian who was present was deeply touched and asked to know more about this God who had moved so wonderfully in George's life.

Sharon had known George since he'd first found the Lord. She had been brought up in a Christian home and had put her faith in Christ at a very early age, but she always felt inferior to George because she didn't have a "testimony." Sometimes she was almost sorry that she lacked a sinful background so she could share how Christ had saved her from it. Yet Christian friends often came to her for encouragement, attracted by her experiences of God working in her life, and non-Christians were drawn to the practical reality of her faith.

"We speak of what we know."

—JOHN 3:11

Many of us think that if we don't have a deeply sinful past like George, we don't have a "testimony." But a testimony is simply telling the story of what God has done for us. It might be how God saved us dramatically, how Christ first became a reality for us, or how he faithfully kept us from the many temptations of our growing-up years. It can also be what God is doing in us and for us at the present time. Even the example of our lives can be a powerful testimony without our saying very much at all.

In Acts 26, Paul includes in his testimony his sinful past as a persecutor, his transforming encounter with the risen Christ, and what God is still doing through him. As you work through this study, ask the Holy Spirit to show you what he has done and is doing in your life that you can share as part of your "story."

PREPARING HEART AND MIND

- What "stories" do you have of God working in your life?

- Have you ever thought of these stories as your "testimony?"

- How would you describe to someone the evidence that God is in your life?

engaging the text

setting the stage

- Paul is arrested and charged with bringing a Gentile into the inner court of the temple, which is forbidden to the uncircumcised on pain of death.

- He is on what turns out to be his last visit to Jerusalem, to deliver an offering to the poor in the church of Jerusalem from the Gentile churches he has founded elsewhere.

- He is rescued by the Roman authorities from a Jewish mob.

- After being transferred to Caesarea, he has exercised his right as a Roman citizen to appeal to Caesar to hear his case rather than be handed over to the Jews, who are planning to murder him without a trial.

- Festus is the Roman procurator (governor) of Judea at this time. King Agrippa is the son of Herod Agrippa (Acts 12) and the great grandson of Herod the Great (Matthew 2). He rules territories north and northeast of Palestine, which are under Roman sovereignty.

Read Acts 26:1–29

1. As you consider the different members of Paul's audience, do you think he was more concerned with Festus and Agrippa, or with the others who were listening as well? Explain.

2. What might Paul's intention be in addressing Agrippa as he does in verses 2–3?

3. What can you learn from Paul here in terms of how you treat those with whom you share your testimony?

Fishing Lessons

"Come, follow me," Jesus said, "and I will make you fishers of men" (Mark 1:17).

When we are transformed by God and start living for him, we become the "bait" that attracts people to Jesus Christ. Within a few hours of meeting Jesus, the woman at the well (John 4:4–41) was telling everyone she knew about what he had done in her life. She had no evangelism training and had never even seen a Bible. But her enthusiastic expression of the evidence led many of her fellow Samaritans to be converted.

The wife of a California highway patrolman was equally enthusiastic when she gave her life to Jesus Christ, but her husband didn't want to hear about it. So she decided to say nothing, and she expressed her love for Jesus by serving her husband—including placing love notes in his lunch box. He told her, "Honey, I don't know what's happened to you, but don't stop!" He was too proud to ask her questions, so he secretly began inquiring about Jesus and eventually came to faith himself.

Enthusiasm for Jesus Christ and a lifestyle of love are both potent "lures" for the gospel. Someone may dismiss a new convert's words, but they cannot deny the testimony of a changed life. Our lifestyle will either validate or deny the message we proclaim.

Do your enthusiasm and lifestyle draw others to Jesus? If not, ask Jesus to transform you so they will!

4. Paul spends some time explaining his upbringing and early influences. Why do you think he includes each of the things he does?

5. Consider how Paul presents his activity as a persecutor. What details does he include?

6. What details of your own testimony might be helpful or distracting when you share it?

7. How does Paul describe his conversion and the further work of God in his life?

8. Identify key elements of the gospel message which Paul includes in his testimony.

9. Describe how Festus reacts to Paul's message and the way Paul deals with this (vv. 24–27).

The Power of Our Testimony

Read Acts 22:1–21.

People can dispute what we believe, but they can't easily deny our firsthand declaration of what Jesus Christ has done for us. Our testimony carries enormous power in bringing others to Jesus and in opening a way for us to speak to those who initially oppose us. Paul recognized this. So, rather than preaching to a hostile crowd about Jesus, he shared his testimony.

Another person whose declaration has won scores of people to Jesus Christ is Gulshan Esther, a former Muslim (see article on "World Religions and Cults," page 00). When she accepted Jesus as her Savior and Lord, her family and neighbors opposed her faith, but they couldn't deny the miracle they saw in her. Her book, *The Torn Veil*, tells how she was left lame by a childhood illness. Then, in bitter grief over her father's death, she asked God for death too. The gentle voice that answered was Jesus, who healed her crippled legs and transformed her life with his love.

Our experiences demonstrate that our God and his responsiveness to us are both real. They affirm that what we say about Jesus is true.

What examples can you share of how God has demonstrated his care and concern for you?

10. What can you learn from Paul about how to respond to possible attacks when you share your testimony?

11. In what way is Agrippa's response different from that of Festus?

12. What does Paul's response to Agrippa show us about Paul's heart in sharing the gospel?

13. When you think of your own testimony (or story), how would you now want to change the way you tell it?

Contemplate what God has done in your life, as well as what he has done through you. Spend some time in worship and thanksgiving to him for his goodness and love.

they overcame him . . . by the word of their testimony.

Revelation 12:11

taking it further

Suggestions for application

DIGGING DEEPER

For further Scripture passages about sharing our testimony, read:

> Daniel 4:1–37;
> 1 John 1:1–4;
> Revelation 12:11.

Meditation

Read about Polycarp of Smyrna on the next page. Meditate on his testimony of God's faithfulness to him just before he died. Think about how you could testify in a similar way to God's hand in your life.

Meditation

Read another account of Paul's testimony in Acts 22:3–21. Compare it with the one we have looked at in this study. What elements are the same? What are different? Think about what might have made the difference in what he shared on each occasion.

Connecting to Life

Write out your testimony—that is, tell your story—in a form that you could use in a conversation to explain your faith clearly to someone. From what we have seen in this study, think about the elements that should be in it and what should not. Prayerfully consider a non-Christian with whom you could share it, and find an opportunity to do that.

PEOPLE OF IMPACT

polycarp of smyrna (c. 69–155)

God Has Never Done Me Wrong.

"Torch him!" Shouting from the frenzied crowd drowned out all but the initial whoosh of the flames as they engulfed the robe of the eighty-six-year-old Bishop of Smyrna. News of the execution spread as rapidly as the flames. Soon everyone in the marketplace knew that Polycarp had been martyred.

The officials, landowners, fruit sellers, blacksmiths, and slaves who made up his thriving church were heartbroken over the loss of their spiritual father. As the last living link to the original apostles, he had faithfully passed on to them the biblical truths and values he had learned from the apostle John. For years Polycarp boldly proclaimed the message of Jesus Christ, establishing churches throughout Asia Minor (present-day Turkey). When persecution swept the region, Polycarp was targeted—on the premise that if the man could be broken, so could the church.

But Polycarp didn't break. When soldiers came to arrest him, the kindly bishop showed them hospitality. When dragged into the public square, he was offered his life in exchange for confessing Caesar as Lord. His response continues to reverberate through the centuries: "Eighty-six years I have been his servant, and he has never done me wrong. How then can I blaspheme my Savior and my King?"

Up Close and Personal
John 3:1–21; 19:38–42

"Of course you're Christians. You're from the West." Andrei showed little interest when Steve and Gretchen first told him of their Christian faith. They were on a trip with the specific purpose of friendship evangelism in what was then the Soviet Union ruled by the Communist Party. They had met Andrei in a park and sat listening to him. Perhaps he wasn't curious about them, but they were learning from him as they asked about his life and family. Finally in a bored tone Andrei asked, "So everyone is a Christian in the West, right? You were born into Christian families?" Gretchen agreed that this was true for her—in fact, her father was a pastor in New Zealand. But Steve said, "No, actually I used to be a communist." Andrei was stunned. "What happened?" he blurted out.

We try to persuade men.

— 2 Corinthians 5:11

It had taken time to get to this point in the conversation, but Gretchen and Steve had shown Andrei respect, taking an attentive interest in his life. That increased his willingness to hear from them. Then Steve's background had "hooked" him. Andrei could imagine a Christian becoming a communist, but not a communist becoming a Christian. Steve related his story to a very interested Andrei, and they were then able to explain the gospel freely to him.

Sharing one on one involves listening and showing respect—treating others as we ourselves would want to be treated. After all, we want them to listen to us. It also means sharing in such a way that people will be drawn to our message. As you go through this study, ask the Holy Spirit to teach you how to communicate your faith more effectively in your personal contacts.

- When you have an opportunity to share your faith with someone, how do you feel and how do you respond?

- What do you think are the differences between "mass evangelism" and "friendship evangelism"?

engaging the text

setting the stage

- It is in the early days of Jesus' ministry.

- The Pharisees are a leading group of the Jews focused on the correct observance of the law of Moses as well as many man-made traditions. Observance of these laws and traditions is seen as the way to win favor with God.

- Opposition to Jesus among the Pharisees and other religious Jewish leaders has already begun to develop, which is probably why Nicodemus comes to Jesus by night, so that he won't be recognized.

- Nicodemus is a highly regarded Pharisee and member of the Sanhedrin—the supreme Jewish council. Jesus refers to him with the respectful title, "Israel's teacher."

Read John 3:1–21

1. Considering the way Nicodemus begins the conversation, why do you think he comes to Jesus?

2. Think of a time when someone initiated a conversation with you about your faith. What do you think led them to do that? What kind of things make us approachable and attractive to a nonbeliever?

3. How does Jesus get Nicodemus's attention?

4. When you've shared your faith, what things have made the difference in gaining or losing your listener's attention? How can you be sure you haven't lost their attention?

Be On the Lookout

As Lisa stood in line at the market, she couldn't help but notice the harried mother and whining two-year-old in front of her. She grew increasingly frustrated with the delay their conflict was causing. Then Lisa heard the Holy Spirit whisper that he hadn't brought her there solely for groceries. He wanted her to bring a touch of his love to this woman.

Lisa smiled sympathetically and helped distract the child. As the mother relaxed, Lisa admitted her own frustration when her child would misbehave in public. "What do you do?" she asked. Lisa explained how she would ask God for his wisdom and patience. The young mother softened and smiled. "Thanks, I'll think about that!"

God doesn't want us to force the gospel on people, but he does expect us to look for opportunities to present his message. Lisa responded to this opportunity to plant a seed. Other times God may want us to harvest. A man named Danny once found himself seated on a plane with an elderly man who had been diagnosed with terminal cancer. As the man poured his heart out, Danny gently addressed his fears by telling of the security of knowing God as the loving Father and all-powerful Lord. Right there the man gave his heart to God!

How prepared are you to use the "divine appointments" God gives you?

5. What do we see here concerning Jesus' attitude toward Nicodemus? (See Setting the Stage.)

6. Sometimes we can be offensive in the way we present the gospel. To show respect is, according to the *Concise Oxford Dictionary of Current English*, to "avoid degrading or insulting or injuring or . . . interrupting, treat with consideration . . ." In what ways can you demonstrate respect to those with whom you share?

7. Jesus does not begin sharing the gospel message until well into the conversation (vv. 10–21). Why do you think he waits this long?

8. What about Jesus' approach would help you in choosing the right moment to bring the gospel message into a conversation?

Conversation Starters

Often the hardest thing in friendship evangelism is knowing how to begin a conversation. Below are a few tips about how to do this. They are not formulas but simply suggestions which many have found helpful in getting over that first hurdle on the way to sharing the gospel.

- When Jesus met the woman at the well, he began a conversation by asking her for help (John 4:7). A similar approach could be: "I've been sent out on the streets today. Can you help me?"
- Perhaps you have known someone for a long time but never shared the gospel or your testimony. A suggestion: "Would you please forgive me for never telling you about the most important thing in my life?"
- When you meet someone on a bus, train, or airplane, one (bold) approach could be: "Did you know that I could tell you something that would change your life, but if I told you, you wouldn't believe me?" Then wait until they ask you what it is!

9. How would you describe the difference between Jesus' understanding of the character of God, and Nicodemus's understanding (see Setting the Stage)?

10. Where is the good news for Nicodemus in what Jesus tells him? How would it change his life and circumstances if he believed?

Read John 19:38–42

11. From this passage, what has changed in Nicodemus since he visited Jesus?

"Preach the Word; be prepared in season and out of season; correct, rebuke and encourage—with great patience and careful instruction." (2 Timothy 4:2)

12. The power of the gospel changes people. Think of someone you know who doesn't yet know Jesus. What might that person be like if he or she were to come to know him? Just as the power of the gospel changed Nicodemus, so it can also change _____ (fill in the name of the person you have in mind).

13. How does this perspective give you hope also for others you know who need the good news and power of the gospel?

Pray for _____ (the person whose name you included in Question 12).

you are a letter from christ read by everyone.

2 Corinthians 3:3 (paraphrase)

taking it further

Suggestions for application

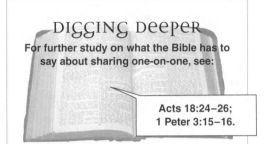

DIGGING DEEPER

For further study on what the Bible has to say about sharing one-on-one, see:

Acts 18:24–26;
1 Peter 3:15–16.

Meditation

Read John 4:4–26, 39–42 and then think through the following questions:

1. What are the elements that make Jesus' sharing effective with the Samaritan woman?
2. What catches her interest?
3. What makes her open up to Jesus?
4. In what ways does Jesus identify with her?
5. In what ways does he distance himself from her?
6. What can you learn from this about sharing with others?

WORLD FOCUS

Read the "People Profile" on the next two pages about the Zhuang people group of China. Take time to pray for them and for missionaries to go to them to share the goodness of our King, Jesus. Refer to "Prayer Strategies for Changing Nations" on pages 103–5 for helpful prayer suggestions.

Connecting to Life

Get together with one or two other group members or friends and create a role play in which you can practice sharing the gospel with a non-Christian. (For example, one person poses as a work colleague whom you meet at coffee breaks who knows nothing about Jesus. Imaginatively play out how you could turn the conversation to the gospel.)

PEOPLE PROFILE

the zhuang—still yoked to legends of their culture

Location: China. Population: 16 million. Religion: 80% Animist.

Daji Mei and her granddaughters selected the most beautiful branches of maple and willow from the bundles lying beside the oxen's stall. They carefully wound them around the posts until the stall looked like a small planting of trees. Daji Mei had decorated this stall as long as she could remember, but only on the birthday of King Ox.

On the eighth day of the fourth lunar month, each Zhuang family would remember King Ox, the ancestor of all the Zhuang oxen. Long ago, the Zhuang farmers had no alternative but to shoulder their own plows to dig their fields. King Ox volunteered to wear the plow yoke in place of the Zhuang men and instructed his ox children to accept the yoke after him. His dedication and loyalty to the Zhuang is commemorated each year by decorating the stalls, giving oxen a holiday, and hand-feeding them with special glutinous rice and delicacies. It is a time to celebrate the ox's goodness to the Zhuang.

Zhuang are familiar with the goodness of King Ox and his offspring; his name is immortalized in their folktales. Yet few Zhuang have heard of the goodness of King Jesus—of how he stooped low, bending his neck to take upon himself the yoke of our sin and guilt. Just as King Ox relieved the Zhuang of a heavy physical burden, King Jesus offers to relieve the burden of sin from any who accept his offer of salvation.

Pray that:

- Many Zhuang would become yoked with Jesus, allowing him to carry the weight of their sin.
- The Zhuang would not be restricted to celebrating King Ox, but the knowledge of King Jesus would permeate their villages.
- The elders and grandparents would embroider the story of King Jesus into the fabric of Zhuang lore, telling tales of his kingdom to their children.

for all Peoples
Romans 15:7–33

Eric was an avid student of biblical prophecy. He eagerly read each new book on the subject and scanned the newspaper headlines for signs of the Lord bringing history to a conclusion and his imminent return. It was an exciting time to be alive.

Then one day he was struck by Jesus' words in Matthew, "And then the end will come." When would that be? Somehow he'd never noticed the beginning of the verse before: the gospel would *first* be "preached in the whole world as a testimony to all nations" (Matthew 24:14). *Only then* would the end come! He knew from his pastor's teaching that "nations" meant "ethnic groups." Could it be that the timing of the Lord's return wasn't just in God's hands? Did it depend to some extent on the obedience of God's people, people like himself, to carry the "gospel of the kingdom" to all the ethnic groups who had not yet heard it?

> **"Therefore go and make disciples of all nations."**
>
> **—matthew 28:19**

Eric's life was never the same after that day. He began praying with new fire for the missionaries of his church. He increased his financial giving to missions. After a time he sensed God's call to go himself. Today he works in a missionary organization outside of his home country, mobilizing and training young people to go and proclaim the gospel to the unreached. He still longs for the Lord's return, but he is now doing his part to "speed its coming" (2 Peter 3:12).

Even if we're not called like Eric to leave our home countries, God wants our concern for others to go far beyond our network of acquaintances. He longs to share with us his heart of love for all the peoples around the world who have never heard his name.

In this passage of Romans we look at ways in which Paul expects the Roman church to be concerned with the "frontiers" of missions in his time. His words are still valid for us today. As you go through this study, ask the Holy Spirit to touch your heart and broaden your vision for the world he wants to reach.

PREPARING HEART AND MIND

- When you think of missions or missionaries, what comes to your mind?

- In what ways are you involved in promoting world missions?

- What might keep you from going into missions, even if you sensed God was calling you there?

engaging the text

setting the stage

- The church in Rome is composed of both Jews and Gentiles.

- A Gentile is anyone who is not a Jew. The vast majority of unconverted Gentiles are worshipers of pagan gods, and immorality is part of their normal life.

- Some Gentiles have converted to faith in the God of the Jews, though they are not circumcised and so are not Jews. These have been especially receptive to Paul's message.

- Paul is a missionary sent out to the nations (Gentiles).

- Spain is the far western boundary of the Roman Empire and is pagan and underdeveloped. No Jews from Spain are mentioned at Pentecost (Acts 2). It is the "frontier" of the spread of the gospel.

- At the time of writing, Paul is on his way to Jerusalem, where he is arrested and sent for trial to Rome. Some traditions claim that he is later freed from this "first" imprisonment and ultimately preaches the gospel in Spain.

Read Romans 15:7–33

1. Paul says that Christ "has become a servant of the Jews" (v. 8). The Jews have often been called "the chosen people." What does Paul indicate they are chosen for?

2. We see that the responsibility of the people of God (the Jews) is to tell the nations (the Gentiles) about Jesus. We as Christians have now stepped into this responsibility. In what ways is your church involved in this responsibility?

3. Paul as a missionary holds the local church in high respect (see verses 13–14; also implied in verses 23 and 32). How would you feel about being described in such a way by the apostle?

4. What motivates Paul's ambition and calling to the nations (vv. 15–20)?

A Reason for God's Blessing

One of the reasons God blesses us is so we can be a blessing, making known his salvation among the nations.

For example, when Christians in Burma were first asked to send out missionaries to the tribes around them, many said they could not become involved because they had no money. However, God reminded them of the rice he provided for their daily needs, and they began setting aside a small portion (uncooked) from every meal. At the end of each week, they sold the rice they had saved, and the amount they earned became their missions offering.

Meditate on Psalm 67 and consider how the nations will respond to God when we share his blessing.

5. This passage, part of Paul's letter to the church in Rome, is like an early "missionary newsletter." Paul brings a number of needs to the attention of the Roman church. What are these needs?

What do you think his goal is in writing about them?

6. Paul's vision is broad, encompassing both home and the nations. Identify some needs and difficult circumstances that you are aware of beyond your own city or nation. Consult the world map on page 106 to help you.

7. When a missionary speaks in your church, shares his vision or calling, and asks for support, how do you feel? Explain why.

- Manipulated
- Excited
- Bored
- Scared
- Ready to go
- Other:

8. Paul's calling is "to boldly go where no one has gone before" — or rather, "where Christ is not known" (v. 20). Think of missionaries who have helped you to grasp the challenge and fulfillment that there is in doing this. What was it that caught your imagination?

9. Before Paul heads off for Rome and then the missions frontier of Spain, he returns to Jerusalem. What is he going to do there, and what can we learn from his example?

Where the Need Is Greatest

A well-intentioned friend said to an aspiring missionary, "How can you even think of going overseas? Can't you see how much need there is right here?" The questions reverberated in the young man's heart. He knew there was great need in his own home state, but still he believed that God was calling him to Asia.

As he prayed about what to do, in his mind's eye he saw a fallen tree trunk. He sensed that it needed to be moved urgently. Then he noticed that there were ten people gathered around the huge trunk, far too few to move it. To his surprise, nine were at the near end and only one at the far end. Both were calling him to help them. The nine needed help, but the one by himself needed help even more. Then he understood: God was calling him to the place of greatest need.

In this same spirit Paul said, "It has always been my ambition to preach the gospel where Christ was not known, so that I would not be building on someone else's foundation" (Romans 15:20). His words were not an expression of independence, but of strategic obedience to God "who wants all men to be saved" (1 Timothy 2:4).

Will you help on the lonely end of the tree trunk, proclaiming the gospel of Jesus Christ where he is not known?

10. Everyone is called! Do you believe your calling is to stay close to home, or to go to the nations? Explain.

11. In light of your answer to Question 10, in what ways can Paul be an example to you, whichever way God is leading you?

12. In what ways have your own attitudes about missions changed as a result of this study? How might they still need to change?

responding to god

Ask the Lord to give you a heart for the world. Look for opportunities and consider ways you can be a world changer.

go into
all the world
and preach
the good news
to all creation.

Mark 16:15

taking it further

Suggestions for application

DIGGING Deeper

Many see missions as the key theme of the whole Bible, including the Old Testament. With this thought in mind, read:

Genesis 12:1–3; Psalm 67; Isaiah 49:6; Matthew 24:14; 28:18–20; Mark 16:15–18.

Connecting to Life

Missionaries are often in danger from hostile people or environments. Paul's request for prayer is an illustration of the need missionaries have for prayer support from those who stay at home. Arrange to receive the newsletter of one of the missionaries from your church or somewhere else. Commit yourself to give to them and to pray regularly for them.

Personal Expression

Do something to bless a missionary or missionaries you know of, whether a single, a couple, or a family. Most missionaries live daily with what might be considered small, but real, sacrifices of things that we may take for granted. Create a personal card (or cards for each family member) to send. Ask their families or mission board what would be an appropriate "care package" of things from home that they might enjoy. Gather those things together and send the package.

WORLD FOCUS

Investigate some of the information available on missions, using the resources suggested in "Missions Resources" on the next two pages. Ask God how he would like you to be further involved in missions.

MISSIONS RESOURCES

AD2000 & Beyond Movement, 2860 South Circle Drive, Suite 2112, Colorado Springs, CO 80906 Publishes the *Joshua Project 2000, List of Unreached Peoples*. Visit their web site: http://www.ad2000.org

Adopt-a-People Clearinghouse, Box 17490, Colorado Springs, CO 80935-7490 Distributes glossy cards with text, photos and maps; profiles of "unreached and adoptable" peoples; and passport-size country profiles on a limited number of people groups. E-mail: aapc@xc.org for more information or visit web site: http: www.aapc.net. Phone: 719-574-7001; fax 719-574-7005

Bethany World Prayer Center, 13855 Plank Road, Baker, LA 70714. For comprehensive profiles of unreached peoples on the internet, visit their web site: http://www.bethany.com or e-mail upg@bethany.com. See "Christian Information Network" below to order paper copies.

Brigada, Online missions resources and weekly e-mail newsletter. Visit web site http://www.brigada.org. For a free subscription of Brigada's weekly missions publication, write: brigada-today-subscribe@egroups.com

Caleb Project Resources, 10 W. Dry Creek Circle, Littleton, CO 80120-4413. Distributes videos; people group prayer guides; gateway cities prayer profile video; prayer cards; church resources (speakers, skits, etc.); handbooks/manuals for researching unreached people groups. Phone: 303-730-4170, ext. 332; fax: 303-730-4177; e-mail: info@cproject.com or visit web site at http://www.calebproject.org

Christian Information Network, 11025 State Hwy. 83, Colorado Springs, CO 80921-3623 Can order the whole set of people profiles produced by Bethany World Prayer Center. Call 888-772-9104 or e-mail Lkayes@CIN1040.net

Frontier Missions International Coordinating Office (FMICO) of Youth With A Mission. Highfield Oval, Ambrose Lane, Harpenden, Herts AL5 4BX, England. E-mail ICO@oval.com; fax:1582-463305; web site: http://www.ywamfm.org

Global Mapping International, 7899 Lexington Drive, Suite 200A, Colorado Springs, CO 80920. Offers many missions resources in electronic format, including an electronic version of *Operation World*, overhead transparencies on missions, wall maps, and computer software for missions. Ask for their "Resource Catalog" and newsletter. Phone: 719-531-3599; fax: 719-548-7459; e-mail: info@gmi.org; web site: http://www.gmi.org

U.S. Center for World Mission, 1605 Elizabeth St., Pasadena, CA 91104. Missions mobilization, training, resource, and strategy center. Phone: 626-797-1111. Web site: http://www.uscwm.org. To subscribe to the bulletin of the USCWM, *Mission Frontiers*, visit their web site: http://www.missionfrontiers.org.

WEC International Research Office, Bulstrode, Gerrards Cross, Bucks SL9 8SZ, England. Unique collection of data, articles, surveys, and clippings relating to world evangelization; provides extensive research data for *Operation World*. Email: iro@opwld.demon.co.uk for more information.

William Carey Library, P.O. Box 40129, Pasadena, CA 91004. Phone: 818-798-0819. Books and materials distributor for the US Center for World Mission. To place credit card orders call 1-800-mission or send inquiries to: wcl.webinquiry@uscwm.org

World Christian News & Books, P.O. Box 26479, Colorado Springs, CO 80936. A mail-order discount source for missions books and videos, including *Praying Through the Window* materials. Phone: 888-WCN-NEWS (US only) or 719-442-6409. Write and request catalog. Email: wcn@xc.org

YWAM Publishing, Box 55787, Seattle, WA 98155. Phone: 800-922-2143 (US only) or 425-771-1153; fax: 425-775-2383; e-mail: 75701.2772@compuserve.com

BOOKS

Operation World, Patrick Johnstone, Zondervan Publishing House, Grand Rapids, MI 49530 by arrangement with OM Publishing, fifth edition, 1993. A comprehensive resource guide organized by country, including statistics and descriptive information on countries, people groups, churches, and missions, with guidelines for prayer.

Strongholds of the 10/40 Window, edited by George Otis, Jr. with Mark Brockman. Available from YWAM Publishing.

World Christian Encyclopedia, D. Barrett, G. Kurian, and T. Johnson, Second Edition, Oxford University Press, AD2000.

You Can Change the World, Vol. 1 and 2 (Children's version of *Operation World*), Jill Johnstone, Daphne Spraggett, Zondervan Publishing House, Grand Rapids, MI 49530 by arrangement with WEC International, Fort Washington, PA, 1992.

DAILY PRAYER GUIDES

Personal Prayer Diary and Daily Planner – One unreached people group, needy nation, or world-class city is listed every day, directing your prayers. Includes world maps, statistics, sketches of people, details about the population, religion, percentage of known Christians, world time zones, and information about Youth With A Mission. Contact YWAM Publishing (see above).

Global Prayer Digest, US Center for World Mission, 1605 Elizabeth Street, Pasadena, CA 91104. Write for a sample copy. Phone: 626-797-1111; fax: 626-2263; web site: http>//www.uscwm.org

30-Day Prayer Focus, booklets and videos to guide Christians in daily prayer for Muslims and Hindus. Issues on Buddhism and other religions planned. Contact World Christian News and Books (see above).

Leader's Notes

Leading a Bible study—especially for the first time—can make you feel both nervous and excited. If you are nervous, realize that you are in good company. Many biblical leaders, such as Moses, Joshua, and the apostle Paul, felt nervous and inadequate to lead others (see, for example, 1 Corinthians 2:3). Yet God's grace was sufficient for them, just as it will be for you.

Some excitement is also natural. Your leadership is a gift to the others in the group. Keep in mind, however, that other group members also share responsibility for the group. Your role is simply to stimulate discussion by asking questions and encouraging people to respond. The suggestions below can help you to be an effective leader.

The Role of the Holy Spirit

Always remember that the work of the Holy Spirit is necessary in order for each of us to understand and apply God's Word. Prayer, your prayer for one another, is critical for revelation to take place. You can be assured that God is working in every group member's life. Look for what is stirring in people's hearts. Listen to their statements and questions, and be aware of what they do not say as well as what they do say. Watch God do his work. He will help you lead others and feed you at the same time. May God's blessing be with you.

Preparing to Lead

1. Ask God to help you understand and apply the passage to your own life. Unless this happens, you will not be prepared to lead others.
2. Carefully work through each question in the study guide. Meditate and reflect on the passage as you formulate your answers.

3. Familiarize yourself with the leader's notes for the session. These will help you understand the purpose of the session and will provide valuable information about the questions.
4. Pray for the various members of the group. Ask God to use these studies to help you grow as disciples of Jesus Christ.
5. Before each meeting, make sure each person has a study guide. Encourage them to prepare beforehand for each study.

Leading the Study

Opening (approximately 5 minutes)

1. At the beginning of your first time together, take a little extra time to explain that the Living Encounters are designed for discussions, sharing, and prayer together, not as lectures. Encourage everyone to participate, but realize that some may be hesitant to speak during the first few sessions.
2. Begin on time. If people realize that the study begins on schedule, they will work harder to arrive on time. Open in prayer. You may then want to ask for feedback from one person who has followed through on the "Taking It Further" section from the previous week's study.
3. Read the introduction together. This will orient the group to the passage being studied.

Preparing Heart and Mind (approximately 15 minutes)

1. Although these questions may be considered by individuals beforehand, you are strongly encouraged to begin your group time with them. They are designed to provoke thinking about a topic that is directly related to the study. Anyone who wrestles with one or more of the questions will be better prepared to receive the truth found in the rest of the study.

2. If your time is very limited, encourage your group members to consider one or more of the questions before they arrive. It is not necessary to mention them in your meeting. However, you may want to ask for one person who has already considered the questions to share thoughts about one question with the group before moving on to "Engaging the Text."

Engaging the Text (approximately 50 minutes)

1. This section is a study of one or more passages of Scripture. Read the Scripture portion(s) aloud. You may choose to do this yourself, or you might ask for volunteers.
2. There are normally 10–12 questions, which will take the group through an inductive process of looking at the text. These questions are designed to be used just as they are written. If you wish, you may simply read each one aloud. Or you may prefer to express a question in your own words until it is clearly understood. Unnecessary rewording, however, is not recommended.
3. Don't be afraid of silence. People in the group may need time to think before responding.
4. Avoid answering your own questions. Even an eager group will quickly become passive and silent if they think the leader will do most of the talking.
5. Encourage more than one answer to each question. Ask, "What do the rest of you think?" or "Anyone else?" until several people have had a chance to respond.
6. Try to be affirming whenever possible. Let people know you appreciate their insights into the passage.
7. Never reject an answer. If it is clearly wrong, ask, "Which verse led you to that conclusion?" Or let the group handle the problem by asking them what they think about the question.

8. Avoid going off on tangents. If people wander off course, gently bring them back to the passage being considered.
9. End on time. This will be easier if you control the pace of the discussion by not spending too much time on some questions or too little on others.

Articles

There are several articles in each study that are set off by gray boxes. These offer additional information as well as help to liven up the group time. "Setting the Stage" relates directly to the study of the passage, and questions will refer you to this sidebar when needed. Other gray-boxed articles can further illustrate or apply a principle. Become acquainted with the articles beforehand so that you know what is available. Remember that reading one or more of these articles in the group will add to your meeting time.

Responding to God (approximately 10 minutes)

In every study guide a prayer response is built into the last few minutes of the group time. This is to allow for the Holy Spirit to bring further revelation as well as application of the truths studied into each person's life. Usually there is a suggested way to respond in prayer, but feel free to adjust that as you sense what God is doing.

Taking It Further

You may want to encourage people to do one or more of these suggestions during the week ahead. Perhaps ask one person to share about it at your next time together. Or, depending on your time constraints, you may choose to do some of these activities during your session together.

Many more suggestions and helps are found in the book *Leading Bible Discussions* (InterVarsity Press). Reading it would be well worth your time.

GOD'S HEART FOR THE LOST
Luke 19:1–10

Purpose: For participants to grow in their knowledge of God's love for the lost, and to enable them to experience this in a greater way themselves.

Engaging the Text

Question 1 It is important for participants to understand the point of this question. Jesus, about to carry the weight of the whole world's sin on his shoulders, takes time for one lost sinner. It is a common joke about someone wanting to do good that "he loves humanity—it's people he can't stand," and sadly it is often true. But Jesus isn't only interested in "humanity" in general; he loves people—even a greedy, lost sinner like Zacchaeus.

Question 2 Although some group members may feel insecure or vulnerable with this question, the goal is to help people recognize hindrances that they may have to sharing the gospel. If you have an example from your own life, it may be appropriate to tell them about it and thus encourage others to be open about their experiences also.

Questions 4–5 Jesus was willing to identify with an unpopular sinner, perhaps damaging his own reputation at a critical juncture of his ministry. This tells us something of the depth of love he must have had for this dishonest tax collector. There will be other insights people can gather from the story as well, so let the discussion flow.

Questions 8–10 These questions all hang together. The goal is for participants to realize that the crowd may well accept Zacchaeus *after* his repentance and promise of restitution for what he has done wrong. In contrast, Jesus is willing to reach out to him, show him love, and even risk his reputation by sharing a meal with him *before* he repents.

Responding to God

It may be appropriate to divide the group into twos or threes to share and pray together. Encourage them to pray for each other for a greater measure of God's love for the lost.

Taking It Further

Refer to the explanation of this section in the introduction to the Leader's Notes. While not a requirement, the aim of these suggestions is to help the study have a continuing effect on lives through the following week. Encourage people to choose one or more of the activities which appeal to them. Make it clear that they are not expected to follow through on all the suggestions.

session two

the Best News ever

1 Corinthians 15:1–28

Purpose: To help participants clarify what the message of the gospel is and connect that message more effectively with the lives of the people with whom they share it.

Engaging the Text

Question 1   The essential elements are: Christ died for our sins, was buried, was raised on the third day and seen by eyewitnesses (vv. 3–8); we are saved by grace and live by grace (vv. 9–11); the resurrection of the dead; the destruction of Satan's domain; Jesus' physical return; the establishment of his kingdom (vv. 12–28).

It is not necessary to point out all these elements at this stage. They will become evident as you go through the passage. However, even after just one reading participants should notice that there is more involved in "the gospel" than the truth that Jesus died for our sins, as central and important as this fact is.

Question 2   Paul himself gives a reason in verse 2, but let the group discuss it for themselves. It can be helpful for people to consider why Paul includes each of these elements in the passage.

Question 4   Christ died for our sins, was buried and raised from the dead; he gives us his grace; he is reigning and destroying Satan's dominion; he will return. God expects us to respond by sharing the gospel (v. 2); believing in the message; receiving his grace, both for salvation and to work for him; cooperating with him both in the destruction of Satan's dominion and in spreading his reign.

There may be different understandings of what it means for us to be involved in spreading his kingdom. For some it may mean nothing more than evangelism and missions, that is, winning individuals to surrender to Christ's lordship. Others may see a broader picture where Christians are to be concerned with all of life. Let the discussion flow, but keep participants from becoming sidetracked into discussing eschatology, the last days, or similar subjects, as these are not the focus.

Question 5   Most participants will grasp the first aspect of grace — that we are saved by God's grace, which is demonstrated by Christ's death for our sins and his resurrection. The second aspect which Paul discusses, that the work we do for God is to be done by his grace working with us, may be new for some.

You may want to encourage people to discuss what this might mean practically for themselves. This truth can bring new freedom for some as they begin to apply it to their lives. You may want to mention "Embracing God's Grace," one of the booklets in this series, which could be very helpful for further study and understanding of grace.

Question 7   A number of different answers may be given. The aim is for people to grasp that the Resurrection is proof from God's side that the curse that was placed on us in the garden of Eden for eating the fruit (Genesis 2:16–17) has been removed. The penalty has been paid. Note verses 17 and 22 in particular.

Question 8   There is not necessarily a doctrinally correct answer, although Paul's words indicate that we need to be careful of what we mean if we make such comments as mentioned in the question.

The aim is to provoke discussion on the real significance of the Resurrection.

Question 9 Some participants may have had some past involvement in the occult, or know those who did, and can share how Christ destroyed that power in their lives. Others may know of stories from the mission field. Telling these experiences can broaden people's perspective of the tremendous scope of Christ's victory in this area.

Question 10 It is important for participants to grasp that the Resurrection is not just a future event for us. Elsewhere in Paul's writings he makes it clear that there is a way in which we share in Christ's resurrection today (see Galatians 2:17–21; Ephesians 2:4–7). The Resurrection has implications for us and the world now, in this age. Paul discusses some of that here.

There is a tension between the present reality of what Christ has accomplished and its future fulfillment. He has defeated Satan, yet we see that Satan still has power in this world. The Father has "put everything under his feet," yet we read that Christ must reign "until he has put all his enemies under his feet" (v. 25). It is already, but not yet.

Leon Morris writes, "There is a dynamic meaning to the Greek *basileia* (kingdom); it is 'rule' rather than 'realm' . . . Paul does not speak of battles, or of rulers being dethroned. But he does speak of all rule other than that of Christ, as being rendered completely inoperative. Although this is mentioned after the delivering up of the kingdom, it takes place before it (as the change of tense in the Greek shows)."[1]

Prayer —— Preparing the Way

Acts 4:23–37; 5:12–16

Purpose: To help participants grasp more deeply the importance of prayer when reaching out to the lost, and to stimulate more prayer in their lives.

Engaging the Text

Question 2 Some elements are: The people quote from Scripture; they recognize that God is the one who is truly in control of circumstances; and they proclaim his good character (that he is willing to heal and do miracles for needy people). These statements indicate that the people believe that they can trust God. They declare further that they themselves are willing to be used by God to reach others, and they ask him to give them what they need to do that.

Question 3 Some examples: He is described as being the God of creation; the God of history (the conspiracies of men only accomplish God's purposes); a God of compassion who heals the sick.

Question 4 It is as we remember the one we are praying *to* that we can have confidence in our prayers. People are his creation, so he cares about us; he is able to act on our behalf in history; he does so because of his character of compassion.

Question 5 It is important that participants are helped not only to consider prayer but to pray in a more effective way. The aim of this question is to help them connect the study as practically as possible to their own lives.

Question 7 There are a number of valid answers to this question. One key point for people to grasp is that God is involved with us as we reach out to the lost. We are not dependent on our own resources but need to look to him for what we need. Another point to understand is that the lost have been blinded by the enemy, and prayer helps to open their eyes.

Question 10 The witness of the love they have for one another would be a clear confirmation to onlookers of their message, that God loves the world.

Question 11 The aim is to provoke discussion on ways that our prayer life can and should affect our life as a church.

Question 12 In their prayer the church links asking for boldness in preaching with God doing miracles (vv. 29–30). This is obviously what is now happening.

session four

Sharing Your testimony
Acts 26:1–29

Purpose: To enable participants to understand more fully the power of their testimony and to use it more effectively in sharing their faith.

Engaging the Text

Questions 2 and 3 There may be a number of different suggestions here. It appears that Paul wants to do what he can to make Agrippa responsive to his testimony and the gospel message, by giving him credit for what he knows. The aim of these questions is to draw out the fact that the way we treat people who are listening to us affects how they respond to our message.

Questions 4 and 5 Paul is "establishing his credentials." He knows that with his background, he would not be a "natural" advocate for the gospel. He has been the enemy of the message he is now defending. This type of detail can be an effective way of attracting people's attention, as they wonder what made the difference. It can also give greater credence to the speaker.

In considering the kinds of details of a sinful past you might mention in sharing with someone else, it is important to note that while Paul states clearly what his sin was as a persecutor of the church, he does not go into detailed descriptions of any specific incident. A testimony should focus on what Christ has done rather than on our sin.

Question 7   He is very clear in pointing to Jesus as the source of his conver-
              sion. Paul further speaks of his commission to spread the gospel
              among the Gentiles and how he has carried this out. Still speak-
              ing to Agrippa, he appeals to the Old Testament to back him up,
              knowing that it is an authority Agrippa recognizes (vv. 22–23).

Question 8   In the midst of his "story," Paul's gospel message is very evident.
              Elements of the gospel include: turning from darkness to light;
              freedom from the power of Satan; forgiveness of sins; faith in
              Christ (v. 18); repentance from sin and turning to God, leading
              to good deeds (v. 20).

Question 9   When Festus rejects Paul's message as that of a madman, Paul
              responds calmly, without anger or personal offense. He turns
              to Agrippa, in a sense setting Agrippa on his side. He seems
              fairly certain that Agrippa won't deny the facts about what has
              been happening between Jews and Christians and at least
              some of the events of Jesus' life.

Question 11   Agrippa's response appears to be quiet and reasonable. It
              implies a possible openness to Paul's message, though he is not
              yet ready to accept it.

Question 12   Paul longs for all those present to come to faith in Christ. It is
              interesting to note that the following conversation between
              Festus and Agrippa (vv. 30–32) takes place after they have left
              Paul's presence. There is no record in history of either of them
              becoming Christians, yet their conversation is recorded. The
              indication is that someone else present does at some point
              respond to Paul's appeal and come to Christ.

Responding to God

You may want to have people share together in twos or threes something
that God has done for them. They can then give thanks together.

session five

Up Close and Personal
John 3:1–21; 19:38–42

Purpose: To help participants grow in their skills in friendship evangelism and to understand better the importance of their attitude in approaching people.

Engaging the Text

Question 3 In essence Jesus tells Nicodemus that he really doesn't have any idea what is going on—a shocking thing for such a highly regarded teacher. Jesus is helping Nicodemus to realize that though he is a leading Pharisee, unless God gives him his life and Spirit, he is not able to evaluate Jesus' ministry.

Leon Morris writes, "He hails Jesus as a teacher 'come from God.' We must notice that he sees Jesus as a teacher only, and that he has yet no perception of the real nature of Him whom he sought out."[2]

Question 5 In referring to Nicodemus as "Israel's teacher" Jesus is using a title of honor. Thus in spite of having just said that Nicodemus doesn't understand what is going on, Jesus continues to show him respect. Morris writes, "'The teacher of Israel' points at the very least to preeminence as a teacher. The article ("the" not "a" teacher) may indicate that Nicodemus held some official position, but if so we do not know what it was."[3]

Questions 7 and 8 There could be a number of answers here. The goal is for participants to see that it does make a difference when we converse with people in such a way that we gain their attention before presenting the details of our message. This helps prepare them to be more open to what we will share.

Question 9 Jesus speaks of a God who doesn't seek to condemn the world but rather to save it. In fact, he loves the world so much that he gives his Son. As a Pharisee, Nicodemus sees God as someone whose favor he has to win. Jesus reveals God as a Father who gives us his grace.

Question 11 At a time when Jesus has been executed and his disciples have fled and are in hiding, Nicodemus dares to come publicly with Joseph of Arimathea to ask for Jesus' body. It seems that he has come to a place of daring to identify with Jesus, at a time when that would take particular courage and even when there is seemingly nothing to be gained anymore. Jesus' message has reached him.

Question 12 While this is not a question in the normal sense, it enables participants to connect the story of Nicodemus and his transformation to those around them. Thus they are helped to grasp more deeply the truth that the same gospel message which changes Nicodemus can change those they know.

Responding to God

You may want to have participants share briefly about the person they have named in Question 12. You could pray for those people as a whole group or in twos and threes.

SESSION SIX

For all Peoples
Romans 15:7–33

Purpose: To help participants gain a deeper insight into the missions call upon the church and the place they can have in this call, whether in giving, praying, or going. To stimulate those God is calling into missions to discover and/or respond to that call.

Engaging the Text

Question 1   The aim is to help participants recognize that the Jews were called to be a blessing to the world and to tell the nations about their God, and that God's intentions always included reaching the rest of the world.

Question 2   Should the question come up, make sure it is understood that the intention is not to imply that God now has no future for the Jews. It is simply to have participants examine the responsibility of the church to carry the Good News to the nations of the world.

Question 5   Paul informs the church that he plans to go to Spain and will be expecting them to help him get there (v. 24). He is clearly asking them for financial support. This part of the letter is in essence a missionary support-raising letter. He further indicates that the church in Jerusalem is in financial need, and though the church in Rome might not have an immediate opportunity to give, Paul is probably assuming that they will pray (vv. 25–27). Finally, he asks them to pray for his own safety and protection (vv. 30–32).

All these are needs that missionaries are constantly confronted with: their own financial needs, the needs of others they know, and for protection. Paul is seeking to broaden the vision of the Roman Christians beyond their own needs, making them aware of their responsibility to care for others as well.

Question 6   Take time to respond to this question. Participants are challenged and encouraged to reflect upon the needs of the world beyond their own immediate spheres.

Question 7   There is no "right" answer to this question. The intent is to help participants to think about their own responses to missionaries and to examine these responses in light of the Bible's missions mandate.

Question 9   We see that Paul is not solely concerned with the people living far away on the frontiers of missions, although that is his call. He is concerned about the "home front" as well. Missionaries should never forget the needs of home. At the same time, those called to stay home need to be concerned with missions. They may not be called to go, but they can certainly be involved.

A further point we can learn from his example is that the mission field can also bless home, as the Gentile churches here send an offering to the poor Christians in Jerusalem. In fact, we see this occurring more and more frequently today, as nations that were formerly "receiving" nations are now sending missionaries to what were formerly "sending" nations, now desperately needy for the gospel themselves. For example, there are South Americans from Brazil and Venezuela (formerly missionary "receiving" nations) now working as missionaries in Europe (traditionally "sending" nations). Missions from the developing world are one of the fastest growing missionary activities of our day.

Taking It Further

You may wish to encourage members of the group to do one or more of these activities as ways to help them grow in their understanding of and involvement with missions and the mission field.

HEARING THE VOICE OF GOD

If you know the Lord, you have already heard his voice—it is that inner leading that brought you to him in the first place. Jesus always checked with his Father (John 8:26–29), and so should we; hearing the voice of the heavenly Father is a basic right of every child of God. The following are a number of ways of fine-tuning this experience:

1   **Hearing God's voice is possible for you!**

Don't make guidance complicated. It's actually hard not to hear God if you really want to please and obey him! If you stay humble, he promises to guide you (Proverbs 16:9). Here are three simple steps to help in hearing his voice:

- *Submit* to his lordship. Ask him to help you silence your own thoughts and desires and the opinions of others that may be filling your mind (2 Corinthians 10:5). Even though you have been given a good mind to use, right now you want to hear the thoughts of the Lord, who has the *best* mind (Proverbs 3:5–6).
- *Resist* the enemy, in case he is trying to deceive you at this moment. Use the authority that Jesus Christ has given you to silence the voice of the enemy (Ephesians 6:10–20; James 4:7).
- *Expect* your loving heavenly Father to speak to you. After asking your question, wait for him to answer. He will (Exodus 33:11; Psalm 69:13; John 10:27).

2   **God speaks in different ways**

Allow God to speak to you in the way he chooses. Don't try to dictate to him concerning the guidance methods you prefer. He is Lord—you are his servant (1 Samuel 3:9). So listen with a yielded heart; there is a direct link between yieldedness and hearing. He may choose to speak to you through *his Word*. This could come in your daily reading of the Bible, or he could guide you to a particular verse (Psalm 119:105). He may speak to you through an *audible voice* (Exodus 3:4), through dreams (Matthew 2), or through *visions* (Isaiah 6:1; Revelation 1:12–17). But probably the most common way is through the quiet *inner voice* (Isaiah 30:21).

3	**Acknowledge your sin before God**	Confess any sin. A clean heart is necessary if you want to hear God (Psalm 66:18).
4	**Revisit the scene of God's guidance**	Use the Axhead Principle (see 2 Kings 6). If you seem to have lost your way, go back to the last time you knew the sharp, cutting edge of God's voice. Then obey. The key question is, "Have you obeyed the last thing God has told you to do?"
5	**God can and will speak to you!**	Get your own leading. God will use others to confirm your guidance, but you should also hear from him directly. It can be dangerous to rely on others to get the word of the Lord for you (1 Kings 13).
6	**God will make it clear in his time**	Don't talk about your guidance until God gives you permission to do so. Sometimes this happens immediately; at other times there is a delay. The main purpose of waiting is to avoid four pitfalls: *pride*—because God has spoken to you; *presumption*—by speaking before you have full understanding; *missing God's timing and method*; and *bringing confusion to others*, who also need prepared hearts (Ecclesiastes 3:7; Mark 5:19; Luke 9:36).
7	**Be alert to the signs God provides**	Use the Wise-Men Principle (see Matthew 2). Just as the wise men individually followed the star and were all led to the same Christ, so God will often use two or more spiritually sensitive people to *confirm* what he is telling you (2 Corinthians 13:1).
8	**Discern true guidance from false guidance**	Beware of counterfeits. Of course you have heard of a counterfeit dollar bill. But have you ever heard of a counterfeit paper bag? No. Why not? Because only things of value are worth counterfeiting. Satan has a counterfeit of everything of God that is possible for him to copy (Exodus 7:22; Acts 8:9–11). Counterfeit guidance comes, for example, through Ouija boards, seances, fortune-telling, and astrology (Leviticus 19:26; 20:6; 2 Kings 21:6). The guidance of the Holy Spirit leads you closer to Jesus and into true freedom. Satan's guidance leads you away from God into bondage. One key test for true guidance: Does your leading follow biblical principles? The Holy Spirit never contradicts the Word of God. Confess any sin. A clean heart is necessary if you want to hear God (Psalm 66:18).

9 **Yield your heart completely to the Lord** Opposition from humans is sometimes guidance from God (Acts 21:10–14). The important thing again is yieldedness to the Lord (Daniel 6:6–23; Acts 4:18–21). Rebellion is never of God, but sometimes he asks us to step away from our elders in a way that is not rebellion but part of his plan. Trust that he will show your heart the difference.

10 **God will reveal your calling** Every follower of Jesus has a unique ministry (Romans 12; 1 Corinthians 12; Ephesians 4:11–13; 1 Peter 4:10–11). The more you seek to hear God's voice in detail, the more effective you will be in your own calling. Guidance is not a game—it is serious business where we learn *what* God wants us to do and *how* he wants us to do it. The will of God is doing and saying the right thing in the right place, with the right people at the right time and in the right sequence, under the right leadership, using the right method with the right attitude of heart.

11 **Stay in constant communication with God** Practice hearing God's voice and it becomes easier. It's like picking up the phone and recognizing the voice of your best friend . . . you know that voice because you have heard it so many times before. Compare the young Samuel with the older man Samuel (1 Samuel 3:4–7; 8:7–10; 12:11–18).

12 **God wants a relationship with you!** Relationship is the most important reason for hearing the voice of the Lord. God is not only infinite, but personal. If you don't have communication, you don't have a personal relationship with him. True guidance is getting closer to the Guide. We grow to know the Lord better as he speaks to us; as we listen to him and obey him, we make his heart glad (Exodus 33:11; Matthew 7:24–27).

PRINCIPLES FOR EFFECTIVE INTERCESSION

1 Praise God for who he is, and for the privilege of engaging in the same wonderful ministry as the Lord Jesus (Hebrews 7:25). Praise God for the privilege of cooperating with him in the affairs of humankind through prayer.

2 Make sure your heart is clean before God by having given the Holy Spirit time to convict, should there be any unconfessed sin (Psalm 66:18; 139:23–24).

3 Acknowledge that you can't really pray without the direction and energy of the Holy Spirit (Romans 8:26). Ask God to utterly control you by his Spirit, receive by faith the reality that he does, and thank him (Ephesians 5:18).

4 Deal aggressively with the enemy. Come against him in the all-powerful name of the Lord Jesus Christ and with the "sword of the Spirit"—the Word of God (Ephesians 6:17; James 4:7).

5 Die to your own imaginations, desires, and burdens for what you feel you should pray about (Proverbs 3:5–6; 28:26; Isaiah 55:8).

6 Praise God now in faith for the remarkable prayer meeting you're going to have. He's a remarkable God, and he will do something consistent with his character.

7 Wait before God in silent expectancy, listening for his direction (Psalm 62:5; 81:11–13; Micah 7:7).

8 In obedience and faith, utter what God brings to your mind, believing (John 10:27). Keep asking God for direction, expecting him to give it to you. He will (Psalm 32:8). Make sure you don't move to the next subject until you've given God time to discharge all he wants to say regarding this burden—especially when praying in a group. Be encouraged by the lives of Moses, Daniel, Paul, and Anna, knowing that God gives revelation to those who make intercession a way of life.

9   If possible, have your Bible with you should God want to give you direction or confirmation from it (Psalm 119:105).

10   When God ceases to bring things to your mind for which to pray, finish by praising and thanking him for what he has done, reminding yourself of Romans 11:36: "For from him and through him and to him are all things. To him be the glory forever! Amen."

A WARNING: God knows the weakness of the human heart toward pride. If we speak of what God has revealed and done in intercession, it may lead to committing this sin. God shares his secrets with those who are able to keep them. There may come a time when he definitely prompts us to share, but unless this happens, we should remain silent: "The disciples kept this to themselves, and told no one at that time what they had seen" (Luke 9:36). "Mary treasured up all these things and pondered them in her heart" (Luke 2:19).

Joy Dawson © 1985

We all have an opportunity to affect the course of history. If we pray with clean hearts, regularly and effectively, for the nations, we become history shapers. We are to pray for all nations and to focus primarily on the body of Christ, the church, as God intends her to shape the course of history. This ministry of intercession also prepares her for future authority in his eternal kingdom (2 Chronicles 7:14; Job 12:23; Psalm 2:8–9; Isaiah 56:7; Daniel 7:27; Revelation 2:26–29).

Here are twelve steps to help you pray more effectively.

1

Thank and praise God for who he is and for:
- The privilege of cooperating with him in prayer.
- His involvement already in the nation for which he is leading you to pray (Philemon 4–6).

2

Pray for an unprecedented outpouring of the Holy Spirit upon the church worldwide (Psalm 85:6; Isaiah 64:1–3):
- That God's people would see that there is no substitute for revival, pray persistently, and be prepared for it. Consider these biblical promises for revival: Psalm 102:15–16; Isaiah 41:17–20; 45:8; 52:10; 59:19; 61:11; Hosea 6:3b; Zechariah 10:1.
- That the church would receive revelation of God's awesome holiness and unfathomable love leading to deep repentance, especially of the sins of idolatry, apathy, and disobedience, resulting in a passionate love for the Lord.

3

Pray for unity in the Body of Christ:
- For revelation of the pride and prejudice that separates.
- That reconciliation would result; success depends on it (Matthew 12:25).
- That seeing their need for each other, they would honor and prefer one another.
- That their manifest unity would influence the lost to come to Jesus Christ (John 17:23).

---

4   Pray for leaders (Judges 5:2; Psalm 75:7; Proverbs 8:13–15; 29:18; Ephesians 4:11):
- For spiritual leaders to be raised up who understand the character and ways of God and fear him.
- To receive vision related to the extension of God's kingdom worldwide.
- For righteous leaders to be placed into all spheres of authority and influence (Proverbs 28:2).
- That God would convict unrighteous leaders, and if they persist in sin, overthrow them.

5   Pray that God's Word would have its rightful place:
- As the basis for laws, moral values, and behavior (Psalm 119:126).
- That preachers and teachers would get their messages from God's Word, and live them and teach them (Jeremiah 23:22; 1 Corinthians 4:16–17).

6   Pray that God's people would see that obedience is the key to the Christian life, that God's priorities would become theirs (Psalm 19:11–14; 34:1; Proverbs 8:13; Matthew 4:10, 19; 2 Corinthians 7:1):

- A life of worship, praise, and intercession.
- Time alone with God, getting to know him through his Word, and waiting on him for directions.
- Having a heart burdened for the lost and witnessing to them.
- A biblical understanding and practice of the fear of the Lord that would permeate every believer's life.
- Fulfilling the conditions to be empowered by the Holy Spirit (Ephesians 5:18).

7   Pray for children and youth:
- To have the chance to be born, hear the gospel, and know that God loves them—that deliverance and healing would come to the abused and neglected.
- That God would raise up anointed ministries to teach them the character and ways of God.
- For revival to come among them.

8 Pray for workers:
- To be sent to every nation and from every nation (Matthew 9:38; 28:19–20).
- That every believer would embrace the mandate "Go to the nations," and seek the necessary grace to stay home if God so directs.

9 Pray for an increased effectiveness of the varied media ministries targeted to reach the lost.

10 Engage in spiritual warfare (Matthew 16:18):
- Against satanic attacks on both the church and the unsaved.
- Ask God to reveal principalities dominating nations and cities. Pray against them (Ephesians 6:12–13; James 4:7; Revelation 12:11).

11 Pray for spiritual awakening of the unconverted, motivating them to seek God:
- Salvation of unrighteous leaders.
- Radical conversions of most unlikely people, resulting in powerful ministries.
- Revelation to come to the ignorant and the deceived of Jesus' deity and claims, with resultant conversions.

12 Release faith:
- That your prayers are being answered (John 14:13; 16:24; 2 Peter 3:9)!
- That the nations will fear him. Praise God that he will rebuild his church and appear in his glory (Psalm 102:15–16).

Joy Dawson © 1990

World Map

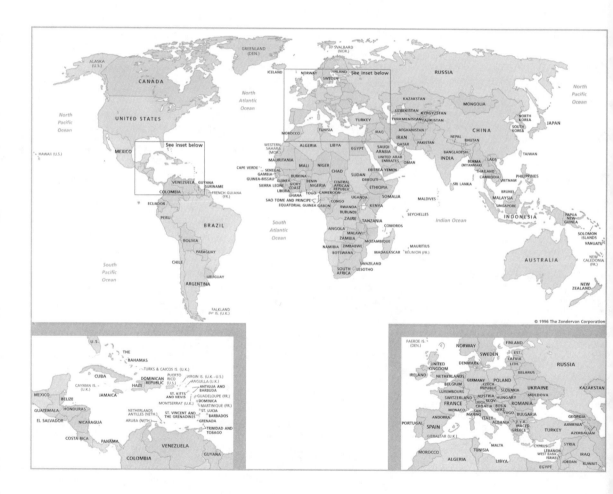

Notes

1. Leon Morris, *The First Epistle of Paul to the Corinthians: An Introduction and Commentary* (Eerdmans, 1985), 211–12.

2. Leon Morris, *The Gospel According to John: the English Text with Introduction, Exposition, and Notes* (Eerdmans, 1971), 211.

3. Ibid, 221.

stay CONNECTED!

Living Encounters Series
Youth With A Mission

Styled after Youth With A Mission's (YWAM) successful Discipleship Training School (DTS), the Living Encounters series draws on YWAM's years of experience and expertise in training people of all ages for international ministry. Its unique, life-changing approach to Bible study will expand your small group's paradigm of Christianity . . . liberate its spiritual passion . . . and fill it with the joy and spiritual vigor that come from following an unpredictable, radical, and totally amazing risen Lord.

Experiencing the Spirit: *Living in the Active Presence of God* 0-310-22706-2
Seeing Jesus: *The Father Made Visible* 0-310-22707-0
Encountering God: *The God You've Always Wanted to Know* 0-310-22708-9
Building Relationships: *Connections for Life* 0-310-22709-7
Embracing God's Grace: *Strength to Face Life's Challenges* 0-310-22229-X
Expanding Your View: *Seeing the World God's Way* 0-310-22704-6
Making God Known: *Offering the Gift of Life* 0-310-22703-8
Finding Your Purpose: *Becoming You Were God Meant to Be* 0-310-22702-X

Look for Living Encounters at your local Christian bookstore.
ZondervanPublishingHouse

About Youth With a Mission

The Heart of Youth With A Mission

Youth With A Mission (YWAM) is an international movement of Christians from many denominations dedicated to presenting Jesus Christ personally to this generation, to mobilizing as many as possible to help in this task, and to training and equipping believers for their part in fulfilling the Great Commission. As Christians of God's Kingdom, we are called to love, worship, and obey our Lord, to love and serve his body, the Church, and to present the whole gospel for the whole man throughout the whole world.

We in Youth With A Mission believe that the Bible is God's inspired and authoritative Word, revealing that Jesus Christ is God's Son; that man is created in God's image; that he created us to have eternal life through Jesus Christ; and that although all men have sinned and come short of God's glory, God has made salvation possible through the death on the cross and resurrection of Jesus Christ.

We believe that repentance, faith, love, and obedience are fitting responses to God's initiative of grace toward us; that God desires all men to be saved and to come to the knowledge of truth; and that the Holy Spirit's power is demonstrated in and through us for the accomplishing of Christ's last commandment: "Go into all the world and preach the good news to all creation" (Mark 16:15).

How Youth With A Mission Works

YWAM embraces three modes of action—ways which we believe God has given us to be a part of the goal of taking the gospel to all the world:

Evangelism — spreading God's message.
Training — preparing workers to reach others.
Mercy Ministries — showing God's love through practical assistance.

Youth With A Mission has a particular mandate for mobilizing and championing the ministry potential of young people. But our worldwide missions force also includes thousands of older people from all kinds of social, cultural, ethnic, and professional backgrounds. Our staff of 12,000 includes people from more than 135 nations and ranges from relatively new Christians to veteran pastors and missionaries.

We are committed to a lifestyle of dependence on God for guidance, financial provision, and holy living. We also affirm a lifestyle of worship, prayer, godly character, hospitality, generosity, servant leadership, team ministry, personal responsibility, and right relationships with one another and our families.

Because of its visionary calling, YWAM does new things in new ways where new initiatives are required. We seek to build bridges among Christian leaders, partnering with local churches and missions for completion of the Great Commission. Annually, over 35,000 people from various churches take part in YWAM's short-term outreach projects.

Teams from Youth With A Mission have now ministered in every country of the world and have ministry centers in 142 nations, but the work is far from complete. We welcome all who want to know God and make him known to join with us in finishing the task — to "make disciples of all nations" (Matthew 28:19).

for more information

For more information about YWAM, please contact YWAM Publishing to obtain YWAM's *Go Manual*, an annual directory of YWAM's addresses and training and service opportunities (send $5 to cover costs), or write one of our field offices for more information. Note: Please mention the Living Encounters Bible study series in your request for information.

YWAM Field Offices

Youth With A Mission
(The Americas Office)
P.O. Box 4600
Tyler, TX 75712 U.S.A.
1–903–882–5591

Youth With A Mission
(Europe, Middle East, & Africa Office)
Highfield Oval, Harpenden
Herts. AL5 4BX
England, U.K.
(44) 1582–463–300

Youth With A Mission
(Pacific & Asia Office)
P.O. Box 7
Mitchell, A.C.T. 2911
Australia
(61) 6–241–5500

YWAM International DTS
(Discipleship Training School) Centre
PF 608
Budapest 62
1399 Hungary
100726.1773@compuserve.com

YWAM Publishing

P.O. Box 55787
Seattle, WA 98155 U.S.A.
Phone: 1–800–922–2143 (U.S. only) or
1–425–771–1153
Fax: 1–425–775–2383
E-mail address:
75701.2772@compuserve.com
Web page:
www.ywampublishing.com

DISCOVER YOUR PERSONAL PATH
TOWARD INTIMACY WITH GOD

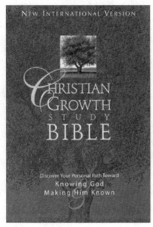

CHRISTIAN GROWTH STUDY BIBLE
New International Version

If you've enjoyed this YWAM study guide, you'll love this YWAM study Bible! The *Christian Growth Study Bible* is designed to help you cultivate heart-to-heart closeness with God. The kind you've longed for and God created you for. A dynamic, growing relationship so vital and life-changing that you can't keep it to yourself—you've got to tell the world about it and help others discover the greatness of your heavenly Father.

Knowing God and Making Him Known is the heartbeat of the *Christian Growth Study Bible*. It's also the heartbeat of Youth With A Mission (YWAM). Which is why this Bible's study program is modeled after YWAM's proven approach in their Discipleship Training Schools. At last, here's a study Bible with a 30-path program that will help you take the uncertainty out of your Christian growth. It helps you determine where you are on the path toward maturity—and helps remove the guesswork about where to go from there.

This *Christian Growth Study Bible* will be an invaluable tool for you to use with your Living Encounters Bible study series, giving you further help on the topics you will be exlploring.

Hardcover	ISBN 0-310-91809X
	ISBN 0-310-918138 Indexed
Softcover	ISBN 0-310-918103
Black Bonded Leather	ISBN 0-310-91812X
	ISBN 0-310-918154 Indexed
Burgundy Bonded Leather	ISBN 0-310-918111
	ISBN 0-310-918146 Indexed